FLY FISHING
CHALLENGE

FORREST OLDHAM

To order additional copies of this book, contact:
Xlibris
1-888-795-4274
www.Xlibris.com
Orders@Xlibris.com

ISBN: Softcover   978-1-7960-7778-0
        Hardcover   978-1-7960-7779-7
        EBook   978-1-7960-7777-3

Print information available on the last page

Rev. date: 01/08/2020

FLY FISHING CHALLENGE

A LIFETIME OF SELF ACHIEVEMENT

Contents

DEDICATIONS

As we journey through life, we encounter other people that affect and effect our lives. I am no different and have been lucky to encounter as a function of my fly-fishing lifestyle many, many wonderful souls that positively influenced me, not only in my fishing, also in the shaping of my character. What follows is an attempt to list not all, as they are too numerous, but some of the significant.

Bruce Summers and Coach Lee were teachers at my High School, the first taught me to tie flies, and the later to cast. Thank you both for the start of a great journey. Jimmy Potter I thank for the rides and enthusiasm to many fishing holes and expanding my circle of waters for chasing anadromous fish. My parents allowed me the pursuit of my fly-fishing interests and the small farm we managed provided some of my early fly-tying materials. Thank you for this.

The American River served as a regular meeting place for many as the anadromous fish and seasons changed to provide us all opportunities to press into action our various skills used to catch the fish. Walt Bennet, Ron Ducey, Larry Cullens, Frank Pullen, Bob Long, Al Perryman, and many others served to help me look to my fly-fishing future and to some degree establish my character. Thanks all listed and those in my thoughts.

Bill Kiene and the "crew" that would hang out at his fly shop were boundless fountains of enthusiasm and information about the processes of fly fishing. Thank you for maintaining the store and the environment needed to keep people on track to enjoy this lifestyle.

Mike Monroe and the group at his store provided not only what I shared in the above paragraph, but encouraged my travel to fish beyond the California border. Mike also refined my fly tying on the back of similar efforts by Andre Puyans. He also shared many wonderful on the water experiences from which I learned much. My sincere thanks.

Many, many more names and experiences come to mind from those encountered on the North California Coast such as Bill Shaadt, Oki, Ted Lindner and other famous or infamous characters.

More currently is a list of CFFU Fly Club members adding to my fly-fishing experience.

Thank you sincerely one and all, mentioned and fondly thought of for all your encounters and assistance.

One more thank you goes out to those pioneers I met only through reading their tomes or from references by the above long list of dedicated characters. I am thinking of those such as Zane Grey, Theodore Gordon, etc. There is also a group of people that have shown up at sports shows by invite to share with the rest of us evidence of on the water experience and enthusiasm. Lefty Kreh, Joan Wulff are two names that come to mind immediately. I invite you the reader to seek all and let them join and enrich your life as a fly fisher as they have immensely done for me.

I really could go on. Let's leave it at a big THANK YOU one and all!

Furthermore, this book is for you, the reader, to help you decide your future as a fly fisher. In writing this my mindset is in helping you establish goals related to fly-fishing to improve your skills as well as your day to day interest in this journey. I wish you great success in this potential life's pursuit.

PREFACE

Surveying the American River with two hander.

I first learned to fly fish when 13 years old. I bought a Wright & McGill fiberglass flyrod with Pfleuger reel and Scientific Anglers 7 weight floating line. Living near the American River, many ponds, and some larger lakes, I pressed into service this combination for quite a variety of fish. I also encountered a lot of other fishers and situations; some a little let's say "slippery" and maybe talked about with trusted friends. All this added up to my "maturing" as a fly fisher for lack of a better word. A lesson learned along the way was to be thoughtful and pondering, not only of the various needs of fishing, also the goings on around me in the wonderful environments our sport finds us. There is also a part of the process dedicated to reminiscing. At some point I, like many before me, asked "What can be done to improve the sport?", and/or "How can I give back?". This is the stage I find myself which is the drive to write this book.

I want to stress that I share my thoughts and experiences for the benefit, I hope, of you the reader, not me. Yet, as I do so, I find the process very rewarding and urge you to, as you get more experience and courage to do so, do likewise. It is my hope this short work helps to set goals for yourself to enjoy this versatile life experience that I have immensely enjoyed. We human beings after all, admit it or not, are goal setters. Some goals are more serious than others, such as getting to the doctor or gas station. Others are "meet as we can" like stopping at the quick market for some item(s) if there is enough time not to be late for some event. The chapters in this book are in similar order to what one goes through in his or her "maturing" as a fly fisher. Each has suggestions for goals to achieve and really can be pursued at any time. The achievement of goals of some chapters can contribute to the possible success of others. An example would be learning to cast well in the wind before aiming at catching many saltwater species. All this in mind, please feel free to read all and keep this nearby for future ideas to set goals to add to your experience in the fly-fishing life.

On a side note, many of the photos feature me. This is due to legal issues relative to others in the photos. You know, model releases and such. I remind you this is for you. If I can do these things, so can you!

TO CATCH A FISH

"Just catch one!"

Some of us at some time encountered a fly fisher gracefully casting away and perhaps most likely catching a trout. This may have been in some wild place or on the tv. The resulting thought would be something like "That looks fun. I want to do that." Some will next go out and purchase something that looks like a fly rod and almost immediately go to test it out, often with frustration, maybe catching a fish, maybe not. The truth is that following the decision to "try to catch a fish with a fly rod.", a goal would be to research and procure the equipment appropriate to catch the desired fish. The next goal would be to find a resource to learn how to use the equipment. Many, now days, will find a number of videos or such online to watch and proceed to incorporate the lessons immediately on the water casting with the thought of catching fish at the same time. I find worrying about catching a fish a distraction to getting a good handle on the management of the casting. One may also find a book or two to help in a similar manner. I do not discourage either, however, I find a good fly-fishing supply with experienced help able to encourage you in your progress to be more productive for most to get a good start on equipment selection and lessons on how to use it. They should also be able to advise you on selection of tackle and gear based on your desired pursuits. In summation finding a good fly-fishing supplier and seeking their advice and instruction probably should be the very first goal!

Author learning to cast two handed rod.

TO CAST

"I just want to learn to cast to catch a fish." is often heard by the fly-casting instructor on the first lesson. It is too bad the new angler has not yet learned the patience the sport will teach you! I do not want to discourage you, just point out there are many casts to learn to adapt to situations you will encounter on the water. Thus, I suggest to you your next goal would include learning not only basic casting, but roll casting, steeple casting, and a couple of casts to deal with the wind!

Ah, the wind! This brings up something a good instructor will inform you of before you set up and wiggle your rod for real. This would be getting some safety equipment! First and foremost a goal should be to get a good pair of polarized sunglasses, an appropriate hat, and maybe comfortable long sleeve shirt. The sunglasses protect your eyes from errant flies that may destroy one of the only two you have as well as help to see into the water better. It should be noted that a sharp knot in a leader may do damage similar as a hook! The hat serves to divert the fly/leader from getting close to your face as well as shade you and your eyes to help with your polarized glasses to see what is going on under the surface of the water. The long sleeve shirt, while not as necessary, will serve to keep out of control casts of flies and mosquitos from inoculating you. As an aside, a better instructor will also show you some tips on rigging and taking care of your "fly-fishing tools" often simply called gear. A bit of serious, regular, practice of your basic casting before going streamside will help you in your goal from the first chapter to catch a fish and maybe more! Further practice and adding to your casting skills should encourage you to bigger and better goals!

In my personal goal setting I spent some time exploring the north coast of California's salmon and steelhead rivers and found unlike my home river, The American, I often had not enough back cast room to effectively reach the fish. Knowing of another fly-casting tool, the two-handed rod, I set a goal to get (make) one and learn to use it for such situations. I have now two such rods and in the process added to another goal, to construct as much of my gear as possible to feel a sense of intimacy with my sport and those pioneers that came before me to enrich the diversity and pleasures derived by my pursuit. I now have additional tools and techniques to further my other goals such as catching various categories of fish.

TO CATCH BIGGER AND BETTER

American River Steelhead from a younger time.

Your focus now likely will be to catch more of what you are now familiar with gaining confidence in using the gear you have perhaps to seek catching larger of the same. Now you may set a goal to discover information about where and how this is possible. Open up your mind to where to look for this information and be willing to talk to others about their experiences. A good follow up with excursions to your best prospects would be suggested. My own experience with this may have been easier than some as I lived near a river with many anadromous fishes that made regular migrations upriver near me. I could take advantage of this to achieve this very goal. In the process your basic skills will likely improve and you may meet others doing the same you may glean insight from! In the process you will likely be catching greater quantities due to your increased skills. These skills can lead to additional experiences and goals!

TO CATCH DIFFERENT

Author travels away from home waters in pursuit of variety. Here a fine salmon from the Smith River. Four flies decorated this fish's mouth.

It will probably be found that the initial gear you acquire can be used to catch more types of fish than you first desired, thus another goal may be to catch a list of a variety of fish! Even today, for me, I discover additional species of fish to pursue. There quite likely are many types near you to catch. You should by now have "tools" to set goals to add to your fly-fishing experience by targeting these and in the process adding techniques that will come handy as you mature in this most wonderful lifestyle. Near me are several trouts, brown, rainbow, and brook to catch. Sunfish as well as three types of bass, and a few anadromous species are also found! Most of these I managed to capture with my first gear, a Wright & McGill 7 weight flyrod, Pflueger fly reel, and a WF-7-F line. I made many adaptations to make all this happen which enlightened me to the fact that additional gear, er, uh, fly rod systems were needed to more effectively catch some of these! I learned to use very heavy flies with mending techniques to get to the depths needed to accomplish my goals. This indicated sinking lines would be a good investment. It was at this time I also spin fished using shad jigs to catch shad. Being creative and having a limited budget I would buy long shaft hooks, split shots, red paint and paint brushes to construct jig bodies by bending the front of the hooks up 90 degrees, clamp on the shot and paint. I further bought various colors of embroidery yarns to match the favorite colors of the jigs used. I used this yarn to crudely tie on tailing pieces of feathers collected from geese and chickens we raised at home. I finished with a couple of half hitches! Being a dedicated and successful angler, others looked to me for their success and often bought these jigs from me! I needed to improve this skill.

TO ACHIEVE PERSONALLY

A small set of steelhead flies tied by the author. One of several tasks
CFFU members show proficiency in for the Coachman Award.

Many fly-fishing clubs have various programs to assist their members in improving their skills. The club I belong to instituted a program some time ago that is quite encompassing and engaging. It is similar to a scouting program having several categories of achievement, casting, tying flies, assisting with club activities or conservation efforts, rod building, and other activities. A participant is asked to display a level of achievement in each category receiving the recognition after completing a specified number. Originally the program was designed for a small group to assist one another using their individual strengths or seeking out for the group others to help the group in acquiring the skills. The entire set of people had to show proficiency or none would get the recognition. The idea was to bring up to a minimum degree the skills needed to be a confident fly-fisher. Perhaps a goal to set would be to find such a club to encourage you on this path. One of the important skills was to be able to tie the several types of flies most will need to catch a variety of fish.

TO TIE A FLY

Author challenges self by tying Atlantic Salmon Fly

You may find you are not satisfied with the flies available to you or perhaps your economy will suggest the need to find a less expensive way to create your flies. Enjoyment of the creative process could motivate you, also, to seek the ability to tie your own. Let me inform you up front, fly tying may not be the expense saver you expect, as you will begin to collect many materials for the process, some a little pricey! You can still enjoy the process. I found I needed faster sinking flies to catch many of the anadromous fish I chased nearby which led me to learn ways to achieve this. I also sought to catch fish in which I needed deer hair bugs, dry flies, nymphs, and streamers. It was fortunate that in the High School I went to there were classes on fly tying and fly casting to participate in if my required schoolwork was up to speed. I made the best of both of these, thankfully! Fly tying, as well as fly-fishing, has taught me many life's skills through the process. I learned patience, process, observation, and practice to name only a few. You may set for yourself an initial goal of learning to tie a few flies to support your previous goals of catching fish which may lead to other goals to be discussed later. I really encourage you to take a good class at a nearby fly-fishing store to get you started. Another path could be through a fly-fishing club, or perhaps by friendship of someone you meet on the water while fishing. Fly fishers are generally very ready to help another. I experienced all of the above and thoroughly enjoy the process even today! You will find there are many, many different patterns created over the years to catch many species of fish in widely differing waters. One of the ways to keep track of these is through books, which incidentally are handy for other reasons. These books will have "recipes" for each of the flies they present. I found myself collecting these books to inspire and challenge me to tie other styles of flies. This collection taught me other things…

TO COLLECT

The author's creative photo displaying pieces of and final construction of familiar Carrie Stevens pattern, The Grey Ghost, often collected.

As an inquisitive kid I collected many things, rocks, bugs, ferns, etc. This carried forward into my fly fishing. I collected several different sizes of fly rods and currently collect vintage fly-tying hooks. Collecting may be an additional pursuit to add to your fly-fishing life. There are those that collect fly fishing books, current and vintage, flies tied by others, current and passed away. Fly tying materials, scarce and vintage, bamboo fly rods, and many other such items are collected. Some of Carrie Stevens' flies may still be available and can sell for $1,000 or more! Many bamboo fly rods are still used even if their price tag is in the thousands of dollars. Their owners often enjoy the character of their flexing or the beauty of the construction. You may be one of these people, or find some other things to collect. Books come in several varieties, humor, fish catching, art and photo tabletop, how to, and reference to name some. I own many in each of the categories. Books are a great way to "stay in the game" due to weather, poor health or some other such thing that prevents you going fishing. I really enjoy some of the humor writings as well as the fishing adventures. I am always amazed by rereading the books in my collection to have "aha" moments given my newer perspective. Periodicals, though not collected a lot are really good for keeping up with new ideas and refreshing the old. Many of the 400 or so club members of the fly club I belong to collect such items and we all benefit from the sharing of various things each knows about our collections. We have a "Vintage Fly" article in our newsletter many contribute to that keeps alive the older techniques and flies of the past. We enjoy bantering back and forth the "facts" we have from our researches on such. This process also builds comradery! Being human, we want to improve and in different ways. There are many ways to take our love of the sport to new levels that our book collection may encourage us to set goals for. One goal to set for yourself is to compete.

TO COMPETE

A prize from Florida waters where the
"Barracuda principle" was formulated. Barracuda are fierce competitors.

I learned a principal from fishing that I apply to much of life I call "The barracuda principle". The concept stems from a fishing trip to the Florida Keys to principally fish for tarpon. On the water there is often down time for the primary species and you often set goals for other catches. There, in the heat of the day and dead calm of the water, we targeted barracuda. We could easily see them hanging over the lighter sand holes between the common greenish ocean bottom. They were usually found as singles. We would cast long skinny bright green flies and strip them back as fast as we could. We soon found out we could not outrace the barracuda with our retrieves and had little real interest from the fish to strike. Occasionally we discovered larger sand spots in which there would be two or three 'cuda. Using the same technique, we now had all the fish chasing each taking it's turn in the lead. All of a sudden one would race forward, often from the rear, to smash the fly! The lesson is about competition!

More than one individual, no matter the species, leads to competition. We humans are only different in that we can compete on intellectual levels in a friendly way! There are fly casting competitions on many levels. Normal length rod to two-handed, male and female categories, distance, style, and accuracy are some of the categories. Our club, at one time, had a contest for fun we called "Float Tube Sharpshooter". A course of floating rings and casting positions was set up to paddle our float tubes about to challenge our casting skills. The person with the fewest casts to the rings was the winner. Additionally, there are fly tying competitions locally, nationally, and within various organizations. They are often set up on different levels of skill, styles or types of flies for different fishes. Fish catching competitions, some of which are large fundraisers, exist, not only for more accepted sport fishes, but for less desired such as carp. An interesting challenge is(are) the "One Fly" contest(s) in which the angler can use only one fly to catch as many or as large a fish as possible to win. Many innovations in fly tying have evolved from this contest to create productive durable flies. One of the fun aspects from the spectator's perspective is the ends to which the participants will go to retrieve their errant flies, caught in trees or bushes, or just plain broken off. If you are the competitive type I suggest you ask around the fly-fishing community or read some of the fly-fishing periodicals for ideas about such. A search online may find one near that you may enjoy participating in. Sometimes the competition may be for the disadvantaged in society.

Banner from one of the community activities CFFU gives back to some less fortunate

The fly club I belong to has for a long time given back to the community in many ways. As mentioned in the chapter on personal achievement the club I belong to has a proficiency program. Perhaps you have a wish to give back by starting similar or other such programs in your club. I suggest getting together with a couple members and brainstorming how one should be set up. A good idea might be to research other clubs' programs to model. Another one I wish to share has gone on for over 10 years and has impacted some of the disadvantaged community greatly. What happens is our club and a few other organizations team up for a day of fishing for some of the community that, through no fault of theirs, are physically or mentally challenged. Some are in wheel chairs or use other methods of mobility. Some just do not see the world the same way you and I do probably. They are brought to the event where there is a small lake or pond that has been recently planted with catchable fish, maybe trout, or catfish. Our club, over the years through asking for donations for such, provides the gear which we, in turn, help the participants use. Another provides the bait or lures. After the time is spent catching the fish yet another group provides a simple lunch for all involved. For a number of years yet another group of photographers wandered about during the fishing making photos of the catches or other such activities. This was good practice for the photo club members! As the photographers produced the photos others downloaded through computers and made medium sized photos which were then mounted on foam core backing to present to the participants. Many really looked forward to their photos! One such I encountered was totally blind! He could not wait to share his experience with others later! The reason for the foam core was some could not have "dangerous" items in their midst. Following lunch there was a ceremony for largest, most, smallest, or whatever other category could be dreamed up with prizes awarded, again donated by yet another group. Everyone went home with something. As some of the participants showed year after year, they arrived with their own fishing gear! For some this event may have been the only time their family visited them. This event, at the same time, totally warmed and broke my heart. I cannot realistically convey to you, the reader, the impact this type of thing has. I would really encourage you to attend and assist such events with whatever skills you have. Who knows? You may find yourself in a position of need at some time and appreciate someone caring enough to help you. There are many other ways to give back. Get involved in Scouting, fishing advocacies, environmental concerns, etc. Just give back to your comfort level or stretch a little.

TO BETTER HEALTH

11,000 FEET & 1/2 OF 11 MILES PLUS

Author and wife at midpoint of a journey towards two goals-
exercise/fresh air and to catch a Golden Trout

Life can and does throw us many challenges. It is likely you will encounter a medical challenge at some point in your life as it has to many, I relayed to you in the previous chapter. It has to me several times! You may set as your goal to achieve better health through the pursuit of your fly fishing. Take my scenario, for instance, in which I was given a new hip joint. I used a walker for many months while the doctors insisted I keep working as they thought my problem was minor back issues. I did not want to give up fly fishing! Ultimately it was discovered my biggest problem was needing a hip replacement. This would be followed by months of rehab. I stayed focused on wanting to continue to fish which gave me the strength to maintain my physical therapy regimen. I also used my rehab time to do tackle maintenance and to tie flies. This also gave me reason to periodically get out of my easy chair to retrieve various needed items instead of vegetating in front of the tv. As I was permitted to extend my ambitions to driving, to see what was going on, I would take moments to walk a bit about the river I often fished. I kept adding in additional distances to where now I can hike most anywhere I need to, sometimes with a little grief. You may find yourself in a similar situation and I would encourage you to look for ways to incorporate your passion into your recovery. Add in longer and longer hikes as you strengthen. Keep your interest up by doing things relative to your love of the sport. Read. I have watched many people over the years have such challenges and many years ago I made it a point to remember places I might go that would allow me to use a wheel chair if I should face similar. I have practiced casting from sitting low positions and with challenging backgrounds that I may have confidence in my ability to do so should the need arise. How dedicated to you are you? I have been very fortunate to fish many places for many types of fish. There are others even more fortunate or better life planners than me that have done plenty more than I. I am satisfied for what I have done, but not satisfied to sit still and not continue. I need to see more and do more!

TO TRAVEL

Coastal Rainbow 8/6/18
Mokelumne River/ Hwy 49

Goose Lake Redband
6/24/18
Lassen Creek

Little Kern Golden
8/20/18
Click's Creek

Fish Creek

Coastal Cutthroat
7/23/18
Redwood Creek

Redband

Collage of photos submitted for first group of two to California's Fish
& Game Heritage Trout Challenge. Saw lot's of California.

Some may be happy with fishing the same place or few places over and over again. To become familiar and good at fishing them, this is not a bad strategy. I, and you also, may need to see more of this wonderful planet we live upon. One of the things I have discovered as a fly fisher is that chasing various fishes has taken me to many interesting places. I set goals for myself to catch some fish that were written about in various books, magazines, and such that encouraged me to travel many hundreds of miles. Encouraged by others and their need to share their experiences with fishes I could not encounter locally and a very good friend of mine's really hard arm twisting I traveled clear across the country. We then left for a "warm-up" session of fishing the flats of the Bahamas for bonefish returning to Florida to catch tarpon. He insisted on a three months "training" in rigorous bad conditions, casting, setting the hook, and following the guides instructions as to where and how far to cast. We pre-rigged flies tied for the trip. I can never thank him enough for this experience. I would not have succeeded as I did without his "training". I subsequently made two other such trips for Tarpon. Today, I am "giving back" by encouraging those willing to go with me to take the California Heritage Trout Challenge. There are a number of groups in our fly club taking up the challenge. I will leave it to the readers to research these sorts of things for themselves.

Just know that many such challenges are being introduced today by various groups or state fish and game departments. Many really wonderful things derive from this pursuit. Firstly, as we set up our group, each of us took on the task of researching the individual species targeted, where they lived, and when best to pursue them. We collectively planned several trips in which we had to, now here comes a good part, travel the four corners of California to catch them! We saw parts of California we never would have seen otherwise. California has, in effect, two such challenges and our group is, as I write this, in pursuit of the second. We are also planning on the Nevada Challenge and talking about other state's challenges as well as the Western States Trout Challenge! Talk about a comradery builder! There are many ways to set goals for yourself and to encourage others to get you out into this wonderful world through your fly-fishing experience.

TO GUIDE

Guide boat on Trinity River. This guide lost most all his gear in a devastating fire, "The Car Fire" in California. We were helping him get re-established by using his service

Another great way to travel, challenge yourself, and give to others is to set a goal to become a guide. Some guides only do so a few months of the year when their favorite fish are most readily available. Others travel many time, climate, and latitude zones to guide everything from high mountain trouts to saltwater flats species, and maybe even exotic tropical fishes in the rain forests. Becoming a guide will definitely be a character former in that you will have to develop your people skills. You may also become a "character" as many famous fly fishers have. There are classes to take to learn many of the skills necessary from boating, to survival, and safety. Safety includes knowing when to back off of a situation for the clients benefit to dealing with nature's curve balls such as itinerant bears. If you like challenges, and have limited home responsibilities, guiding may be for you. You may need other skills as a prerequisite to perform as a guide which may be learned or may already have. An example would be that many Alaskan guides show up to camps early to repair and set up the lodges and such in readiness for the guests. Carpentry, plumbing, roofing, and many other abilities come into play. The same is true for closing down at the end of the season. Any way you look at it rewards will follow! You will have many stories to share with those wanting to listen or compare notes. Guiding combines well as do most previously mentioned skills into many other goals, some of which you may not have thought of.

TO BE AN ARTIST

A playful photograph portraying "Flying Fish"

I belong to two photo organizations as one other passion of mine is to make good photos especially of the outdoors and outdoor activities. Let's get something straight, photography can be and is an art form. This day and age there are many ways to creatively use photography to express one's self. Some may like to paint, sculpt or do who knows what in whatever media with the fly-fishing outdoors theme. Inspiration can easily come from any of the activities expressed in this book. There are a good many people making livings from their work on such things. Some are well known and collected. You may have such a creative mind and could look for ways to incorporate your artistic bent in the fly-fishing lifestyle. I would suggest going to some of the fly-fishing related trade shows and wandering around asking questions of those vendors you may want to emulate. Perhaps a family member is the artist and looking for inspiration.

TO BUILD FAMILY

GOLDEN TROUT

Trio of photos from Golden Trout Expedition-Manzanar Monument left, Golden Trout right

Not all people are interested in fly-fishing which brings up what may be a very important point for you. Most have family members whether only a spouse or perhaps kids, young or out on their own. It can be done with a little thoughtfulness on your part to share the experience with them knowing that it is just that, shared experience. My wife has enjoyed watching me fish without actually participating. However, her passion is both travel and one-armed bandits. As a function of this we plan loosely around the fishing, especially new locations, relatively near casinos. We may do this camping, or staying in one or more of the timeshares we have. We may also invite others along that share similar pursuits. This often works well as the fishing is not always great anyway. You can probably figure this could work for some family time, too. On one of our camping trips the main goal was to catch golden trout, the California state fish. They live only at higher altitudes. First day there I was the victim of altitude sickness and needed to head down for the day to a lower altitude. We visited a larger town for the area and had a nice lunch at a restaurant that doubled as a fine bakery. My wife was in heaven checking out the goods! Later we visited a WW II Japanese internment camp now a museum. Having known a number of Japanese fishing acquaintances and the fact they had been interred in such a place I was brought to tears as I experienced the museum. We both learned a lot and enjoyed the experience. I bought two movies about the experience, one about a photographer named Toyo that was interred there and helped document the experience. The other was a general overview. I also found out the Japanese were so trusted the guards would not only let them sneak out at night, they also provided them with some fishing gear! They were dubbed the Manzanar Fishing Club! The point being there is more to life than just the fishing and it can be combined for a very rich experience for all.

TO WRAP UP

Challenges-Color photos self portraits radio triggered

As you journey as a fly fisher you will face many challenges. Some will be fun and interesting. Some may be serious. I have seen many from hard to catch fish to fishin' rig hazards. Nearly all of my California Heritage Trout trips had car troubles. Power steering pump and pressure lines, and a need for a fresh engine occurred. We, my co-fishers and I, overcame each to catch our trophies! I have many times been able to observe fish, sometimes in great numbers, only to be frustrated in attempts to catch them! Generally, all problems were ultimately solved with perseverance. How will you do?

As I have hopefully pointed out, there is a lot to do as a fly fisher to enjoy your life. There are probably many other ways I have not presented here and I hope you are creative enough to do so in your own way in addition, perhaps, to some of the paths outlined herein. Fly-fishing has been a very enriching part of my life. I have incorporated many of the ideas I presented here into my own life. One of the most fulfilling is the process of "giving back". This is an ongoing pursuit on several fronts, from helping others to improve their casting and fishing skills, to encouraging many to learn of the historical aspects of our wonderful sport through books, collecting, tying and other such activities. This has had me involved with many wonderful individuals and the greatest reward I can receive is, "Thanks Forrest for your helping me with…_____". Fill in the blank! I hope your journey is as rich and perhaps richer than mine!

BONUS-A POEM

What follows is an ongoing work of inspiration that perhaps some of you will understand and appreciate. I do not expect all to do so. The words to this came to me naturally on a trip to my local river with my very young son. I was merely contemplating the beauty of the moment as my son and I wandered about discovering things and watching the sun set with a tremendous flourish of color. I had the insight to write down the words and more came to mind as time went by. The words brought forth pictures in my mind that I have tried to express through the photos with the words. There are a couple messages with one I consider to be of most significance that relates to the preceding work. I would encourage you to let this rattle around a bit in your mind if it does not immediately make sense. The message really is a reflection of my philosophy for life. I hope the message(s) come through to you and I wish you well on your journey.

Floating,sinking, in between the question,
of the reel appreciates machinist's perfections.
Line of pink, green or brown he must decide.
The reel upon the rod he applies.
Hurriedly stringing the rod
Knots hang upon the guides.
Preparations thus far done,
Down dusty trail strides.

With anticipation, excitement, and wonder,
At destination's edge, the Fly Fisher hovers.
Overlooking the watery world below,
Looks through Fly Fisher's eyes.
Sees shades of gray, brown, green, and blue,
In the winding, twisting water as it approaches island wyes.
Pauses to remove from protections
Rod, reel, and flies.

FLY FISHER'S EYES

Out of receptacle metal, leather, or poly,
Selects from covey of flies,
One pondered with critical eye.
Questions, "Will it live up to it's disguise?"
To wispy filament applied,
With twists and turns knot is tied.
Overhead great blue heron flies,
"A fellow fisher...", as it glides.

A moment of hesitation at water's edge
For adjustment of glasses polarized.
Observes shapes and shadows black, gray, green, and brown,
as they undulate, surge, and slowly materialize.
On the surface gossamer tidbits flitter.
Splash! A small drama. An insect dies.
A profusion, a legion, or horde,
For millenia they continue to morphize.

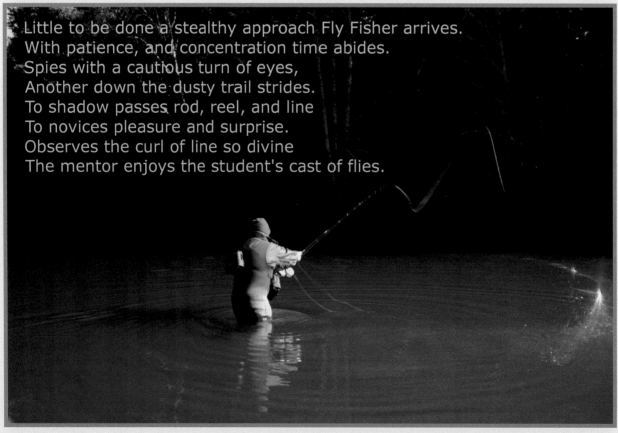

Little to be done a stealthy approach Fly Fisher arrives.
With patience, and concentration time abides.
Spies with a cautious turn of eyes,
Another down the dusty trail strides.
To shadow passes rod, reel, and line
To novices pleasure and surprise.
Observes the curl of line so divine
The mentor enjoys the student's cast of flies.

PERSONAL ACHIEVEMENTS

To comfort the charge,
Imparts lessons from past by the wise.
Shadows lengthen and light lessens
As memories pass as warm as sunrise.
Difficult these images put to paper and pen,
Seen through Fly Fisher's Eyes.
Through time and experience senses open.
Many are the pleasures upon which this person thrives.
Only one of which...is to pass on Fly Fisher's Eyes.

Your place to keep track of your journey !

Printed in the United States
By Bookmasters